PERFECT PICK

A Gift For
$ 3F

From
Si-On Kim

SCHOLASTIC

This book belongs to
Mrs. Fairley

THE ART OF FREEDOM
How Artists See America

by Bob Raczka

MILLBROOK PRESS/MINNEAPOLIS

Jasper Johns • *Map* (1961) • The Museum of Modern Art, New York

America is a country.

America is **an idea**.

John Trumbull • *The Declaration of Independence, 4 July 1776* (1786–1820)
Yale University Art Gallery, New Haven, Connecticut

America is farms.

Paul Seifert • *Wisconsin Farm Scene* (1880) • Fenimore Art Museum, Cooperstown, New York

America is cities.

Berenice Abbott • *The Night View* (ca. 1934)
Museum of the City of New York

Samuel Anderson Robb
Baseball Player (1888–1902)
Heritage Museums & Gardens
Sandwich, Massachusetts

America is baseball.

America is jazz.

Stuart Davis • *The Mellow Pad* (1945–1951) • Brooklyn Museum, New York

America is native peoples.

George Catlin • *Jú-ah-kís-gaw, Woman with Her Child in a Cradle* (1835)
Smithsonian American Art Museum, Washington, D.C.

America is immigrants.

George Bellows • *Cliff Dwellers* (1913) • Los Angeles County Museum of Art, California

America is **black and white**.

William Klein • *Candy Store, New York* (1955)
Howard Greenberg Gallery, New York

America is a rainbow.

Heal
those broken
souls who have
no peace and lead
us all from
darkness into
light

Judy Chicago • *Rainbow Shabbat* (1992) • Collection of the Artist and Through the Flower,
Belen, New Mexico

America is hard work.

Thomas Hart Benton • *Cradling Wheat* (1938) • Saint Louis Art Museum, Missouri

America is sacrifice.

Augustus Saint-Gaudens • *The Robert Gould Shaw Memorial* (1897) • Boston Common, Boston, Massachusetts

America is
natural wonders.

Thomas Moran • *The Grand Canyon of the Yellowstone* (1872)
Smithsonian American Art Museum, Washington, D.C.

America is **man-made marvels.**

Georgia O'Keeffe • *Brooklyn Bridge* (1949)
Brooklyn Museum, New York

America is the open road.

Ansel Adams • *Desert Road, Nevada* (ca.1960)
The Ansel Adams Publishing Rights Trust, Mill Valley, California

America is Main Street.

Edward Hopper • *Early Sunday Morning* (1930) • Whitney Museum of American Art, New York

Mark Tansey • *Action Painting II* (1984) • The Montreal Museum of Fine Arts, Quebec

America is **freedom**.

America is a work in progress.

Gilbert Stuart • *George Washington* (1796) • Museum of Fine Arts, Boston, Massachusetts
National Portrait Gallery, Washington, D.C.

How Artists See America

Jasper Johns (1930–)

Jasper Johns is best known for his paintings of maps, targets, flags, and numbers. When asked what his art means, he once said, "There may or may not be an idea, and the meaning may just be that the painting exists."

Stuart Davis (1892–1964)

The art of Stuart Davis has been described as an American form of Cubism. He was influenced by jazz music, which he loved, and once said, "I think all my paintings, at least in part, come from this influence."

John Trumbull (1756–1843)

In a letter to Thomas Jefferson, John Trumbull once wrote, "The greatest motive . . . for continuing my pursuit of painting has been the wish of commemorating the great events of our country's revolution."

George Catlin (1796–1872)

A self-taught portrait painter, George Catlin wanted to record Native American culture. In 1830, he began visiting various Native American groups, eventually making more than five hundred paintings and sketches.

Paul Seifert (1840–1921)

Born in Germany, Paul Seifert settled in Wisconsin around 1867, where he raised flowers, fruits, and vegetables. He was also a traveling folk painter, who never charged more than $2.50 to paint someone's farm.

George Bellows (1882–1925)

George Bellows sympathized with the poor immigrants who lived in the slums of New York City. In *Cliff Dwellers*, he shows an overcrowded neighborhood on the Lower East Side, where people can't escape from the heat of summer.

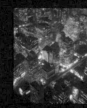

Berenice Abbott (1898–1991)

Berenice Abbott started out as a portrait photographer but became famous for her black-and-white photos of New York City streets and skylines. "I didn't decide to be a photographer," she said. "I just happened to fall into it."

William Klein (1928–)

William Klein's *Candy Store* photo is from his photographic diary of New York City, titled *Life Is Good and Good for You in New York*. Oddly enough, New York publishers rejected it, so he had it published in Paris.

Samuel Anderson Robb (1851–1928)

Samuel Anderson Robb emigrated from Scotland to New York City and became one of the most popular wood sculptors of his time. His carvings of baseball players and Native Americans were used to advertise cigar stores.

Judy Chicago (1939–)

Judy Chicago's art celebrates the power of women. In her stained-glass piece, *Rainbow Shabbat*, a woman gives a traditional Jewish blessing at the head of a table where people of many races and religions are gathered.

Thomas Hart Benton *(1889–1975)*

As a Regionalist mural painter, Thomas Hart Benton wasn't a fan of modern art trends, preferring to paint scenes from rural life. His father was a U.S. Congressman, and his great uncle was a U.S. Senator.

Augustus Saint-Gaudens *(1848–1907)*

The *Shaw Memorial* took Augustus Saint-Gaudens fourteen years to complete. It honors Colonel Robert Gould Shaw, who was white, and his all-African American 54th Massachusetts Volunteer Infantry. In one Civil War battle, Shaw died with 115 of his men.

Thomas Moran *(1837–1926)*

The Grand Canyon of the Yellowstone by Thomas Moran was the first American landscape by an American artist ever purchased by the U. S. government. It paid Moran $10,000 for the painting, which is 7 feet high and 12 feet wide.

Georgia O'Keeffe *(1887–1986)*

Brooklyn Bridge was the last painting Georgia O'Keeffe did before moving from New York to New Mexico. Art historians see it as her good-bye to the city and to her husband, photographer Alfred Stieglitz, who died there.

Ansel Adams *(1902–1984)*

Through his photography, Ansel Adams fell in love with America's natural wonders and became a conservationist. He helped persuade Congress to establish Kings Canyon National Park in 1940, and he was awarded the Presidential Medal of Freedom by Jimmy Carter in 1980.

Edward Hopper *(1882–1967)*

His paintings include many typical American scenes, such as small town streets, gas stations, and railroads. But Edward Hopper once said, "I don't think I ever tried to paint the American Scene; I'm trying to paint myself."

Mark Tansey *(1949–)*

Mark Tansey, whose parents were both art historians, creates paintings that poke fun at both art and history. In *Action Painting II*, we see amateur artists painting the space shuttle liftoff as if it were a landscape or a still life.

Gilbert Stuart *(1755–1828)*

Gilbert Stuart's unfinished portrait of Washington, called the Athenaeum portrait, is the same one we see on the dollar bill. He painted it from life, then used it to make at least seventy-five copies, which he sold for $100 each.

To Jean, who made my dream of being a published author come true

Text copyright © 2008 by Bob Raczka

Millbrook Press
A division of Lerner Publishing Group, Inc.
241 First Avenue North
Minneapolis, MN 55401 U.S.A.

Website address: www.lernerbooks.com

Library of Congress Cataloging-in-Publication Data

Raczka, Bob.
    The art of freedom: how artists see America / by Bob Raczka.
      p.   cm. — (Bob Raczka's art adventures)
    ISBN: 978-0-8225-7508-5 (lib. bdg. : alk. paper)
    1. United States—In art—Juvenile literature. 2. Art, American—Juvenile literature. I. Title.
    N8214.5.U6R33 2008
    704.9'49973—dc22   2007023831

Manufactured in the United States of America
1 2 3 4 5 6 – DP – 13 12 11 10 09 08

Cover art courtesy of: Jasper Johns, *Map*, 1961, 6' 6" x 10' 3 1/8", Oil on canvas, Gift of Mr. and Mrs. Robert C. Scull (277.1963), The Museum of Modern Art. Art © Jasper Johns/Licensed by VAGA, New York, NY. Digital Image © The Museum of Modern Art/Licensed by SCALA/Art Resource, NY.

Interior art courtesy of: Page 2: Jasper Johns, *Map*, 1961, 6' 6" x 10' 3 1/8", Oil on canvas, Gift of Mr. and Mrs. Robert C. Scull (277.1963), The Museum of Modern Art. Art © Jasper Johns/Licensed by VAGA, New York, NY. Digital Image © The Museum of Modern Art/Licensed by SCALA/Art Resource, NY; Page 5: John Trumbull, *The Declaration of Independence, 4 July 1776*, 1786-1820, Oil on canvas, 20 7/8 x 31 in. (53 x 78.7 cm), Trumbull Collection 1832.3, Yale University Art Gallery/Art Resource, NY; Page 6: Fenimore Art Museum, Cooperstown, New York. Photo: Richard Walker; Page 7: © Berenice Abbott/Commerce Graphics Ltd., Inc., NYC. *The Night View*, 1934, Photograph by Berenice Abbott, Museum of the City of New York, Gift of Todd Watts; Page 8: Courtesy Heritage Museums & Gardens, Sandwich, Massachusetts; Page 11: Stuart Davis, *The Mellow Pad*, 1945-51, 66.7x107 cm, Oil on canvas, Brooklyn Museum. Art © Estate of Stuart Davis/Licensed by VAGA, New York, NY. Image © Brooklyn Museum/CORBIS; Page 12: Smithsonian American Art Museum, Washington, DC/Art Resource, NY; Page 13: George Bellows, *Cliff Dwellers*, 1913 (16.4) Los Angeles County Museum of Art, Los Angeles County Fund. Photograph © 2006 Museum Associates/LACMA; Page 15: © William Klein, Courtesy Howard Greenberg Gallery, NYC; Page 16–17: © 2007 Judy Chicago/Artists Rights Society (ARS), New York. *Rainbow Shabbat* from The Holocaust Project: From Darkness into Light, stained glass, 4 ft.x16 in.x16 ft., 1992, fabricated by Bob Gomez, glass painting by Dorothy Maddy. Photo: © Donald Woodman; Page 18: Thomas Hart Benton, *Cradling Wheat*, 1938, 31 1/4 x 39 1/4 in., Tempera and oil on board, Saint Louis Art Museum. Art © Thomas Hart Benton and Rita P. Benton Testamentary Trusts/Licensed by VAGA, New York, NY. Photo: Saint Louis Art Museum, Museum Purchase; Page 19: © Alan Briere/SuperStock; Page 20–21: Lent by the Department of the Interior Museum, Smithsonian American Art Museum, Washington, DC/Art Resource, NY; Page 23: © 2007 Georgia O'Keeffe Museum/Artists Rights Society (ARS), New York. Image © Brooklyn Museum/CORBIS; Page 24: Photograph by Ansel Adams, *Desert Road, Nevada*, ca. 1960 © The Ansel Adams Publishing Rights Trust, Courtesy Collection Center for Creative Photography, University of Arizona; Page 25: © Francis G. Mayer/CORBIS; Page 26: © Mark Tansey, *Action Painting II*, 1984, The Montreal Museum of Fine Arts, gift of Nahum Gelber, Q.C. Photo: The Montreal Museum of Fine Arts, Brian Merrett; Page 29: Gilbert Stuart, American, 1755–1828, *George Washington*, 1796, Oil on canvas, 121.28 x 93.98 cm (47 3/4 x 37 in.), William Francis Warden Fund, John H. and Ernestine A. Payne Fund, Commonwealth Cultural Preservation Trust. Jointly owned by the Museum of Fine Arts, Boston, and the National Portrait Gallery, Washington D.C., 1980.1. Photograph © 2008 Museum of Fine Arts, Boston, Licensed by National Portrait Gallery, Smithsonian Institution/Art Resource, NY.